M. Cottington .

Young Lions

Out of the Blue
An Anthology of Weather Poems

Blood punches through each vein
As lightning strips the window pane . . .

This collection includes poems about all sorts of weather, not just the warm sunny days, but the frosty, sleety, thundry days too. There's a rain picture poem by George Macbeth; a spring sunshine poem by Laurie Lee; a powerful stormy poem by Ted Hughes and many more, each vividly capturing the different moods of the weather.

Other poetry collections published in Young Lions

Hairy Tales and Nursery Crimes *Michael Rosen*
Mind Your Own Business *Michael Rosen and Quentin Blake*
The Lions Book of Young Verse *Julia Watson and Quentin Blake*
A Children's Zoo *Julia Watson and Karen Strachy*
Rabbiting On *Kit Wright and Posy Simmonds*
Salford Road and Other Poems *Gareth Owen*
Song of the City *Gareth Owen*
Toughie Toffee ed. *David Orme*

Out of the Blue
An Anthology of Weather Poems

chosen by
Fiona Waters

with drawings and etchings by Veroni

Young Lions
An Imprint of HarperCollins Publishers

First published in Lions 1982
Third impression February 1992

Lions is an imprint of the Children's Division,
part of HarperCollins Publishers Ltd,
77–85 Fulham Palace Road, Hammersmith,
London W6 8JB

ISBN 0-00-671960-0

Set in Ehrhardt
Printed and bound in Great Britain by
HarperCollins Manufacturing, Glasgow

Contents

This collection is for PMS from FMW
Illustrated by Veroni for Drummond

Weathers
Thomas Hardy

This is the weather the cuckoo likes,
    And so do I;
When showers betumble the chestnut spikes,
    And nestlings fly:
And the little brown nightingale bills his best,
And they sit outside at 'The Travellers' Rest',
And maids come forth sprig-muslin drest,
And citizens dream of the south and west,
    And so do I.

This is the weather the shepherd shuns,
    And so do I;
When beeches drip in browns and duns,
    And thresh, and ply;
And hill-hid tides throb, throe on throe,
And meadow rivulets overflow,
And drops on gate-bars hang in a row,
And rooks in families homeward go,
    And so do I.

The Pedalling Man
Russell Hoban

We put him on the roof and we painted him blue,
And the pedalling man knew what to do –
He just pedalled, yes he pedalled:
He rode through the night with the wind just right
And he rode clear into the morning,
Riding easy, riding breezy, riding
Slow in the sunrise and the wind out of the east.

A weathervane was what he was –
Cast-iron man with a sheet-iron propeller, riding a
Worm gear, holding a little steering wheel,
Iron legs pumping up and down – show him a
Wind and he'd go. Work all day and
All his pay was the weather. Nights, too,
We'd lie in bed and hear him
Creak up there in the dark as he
Swung into the wind and worked up speed,
Humming and thrumming so you could
Feel it all through the house –
The more wind, the faster he went, right through
Spring, summer, and fall.

He rode warm winds out of the south,
Wet winds out of the east, and the
Dry west winds, rode them all with a
Serious iron face. Hard-nosed, tight-mouthed
Yankee-looking kind of an iron man.
"Show me a wind and I'll go," he said.
"I'm a pedalling fool and I'm heading for weather."
The weather came and he kept on going, right into
Winter, and the wind out of the north and no letup –
We lived on a hill, and wind was what we got a lot of.

It's Never Fair Weather

Ogden Nash

I do not like the winter wind
That whistles from the North.
My upper teeth and those beneath
They jitter back and forth.
Oh, some are hanged, and some are skinned,
And others face the winter wind.

I do not like the summer sun
That scorches the horizon.
Though some delight in Fahrenheit,
To me it's deadly pizen.
I think that life would be more fun
Without the simmering summer sun.

I do not like the signs of spring,
The fever and the chills,
The icy mud, the puny bud,
The frozen daffodils.
Let other poets gaily sing;
I do not like the signs of spring.

I do not like the foggy fall
That strips the maples bare;
The radiator's mating call,
The dank, rheumatic air;
I fear that taken all in all,
I do not like the foggy fall.

The winter sun, of course, is kind,
And summer's wind a saviour,
And I'll merrily sing of fall and spring
When they're on their good behaviour.
But otherwise I see no reason
To speak in praise of any season.

Thaw

Edward Thomas

Over the land freckled with snow half-thawed
The speculating rooks at their nests cawed
And saw from elm-tops, delicate as flower of grass,
What we below could not see, Winter pass.

Last Snow

Andrew Young

Although the snow still lingers
Heaped on the ivy's blunt webbed fingers
And painting tree-trunks on one side,
Here in this sunlit ride
The fresh unchristened things appear
Leaf, spathe and stem,
With crumbs of earth clinging to them
To show the way they came
But no flower yet to tell their name,
And one green spear
Stabbing a dead leaf from below
Kills winter at a blow.

'The Fight of the Year'

Roger McGough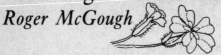

'And there goes the bell for the third month
and Winter comes out of its corner looking groggy
Spring leads with a left to the head
followed by a sharp right to the body

        daffodils
        primroses
        crocuses
        snowdrops
        lilacs
        violets
        pussywillow

Winter can't take much more punishment
and Spring shows no signs of tiring
     tadpoles
     squirrels
     baalambs
     badgers
     bunny rabbits
     mad march hares
     horses and hounds
Spring is merciless
Winter won't go the full twelve rounds
     bobtail clouds
     scallywaggy winds
     the sun
     a pavement artist
     in every town

A left to the chin
and Winter's down!
    tomatoes
    radish
    cucumber
    onions
    beetroot
    celery
    and any
    amount
    of lettuce
    for dinner
Winter's out for the count
Spring is the winner!'

Snowman

Shel Silverstein

'Twas the first day of the springtime,
And the snowman stood alone
As the winter snows were melting,
And the pine trees seemed to groan,
"Ah, you poor sad smiling snowman,
You'll be melting by and by."
Said the snowman, "What a pity,
For I'd like to see July.
Yes, I'd like to see July, and please don't ask me why.
But I'd like to, yes I'd like to, oh I'd like to see July."

Chirped a robin, just arriving,
"Seasons come and seasons go,
And the greatest ice must crumble
When it's flowers' time to grow.
And as one thing is beginning
So another thing must die,
And there's never been a snowman
Who has ever seen July.
No, they never see July, no matter how they try.
No, they never ever, never ever, never see July."

But the snowman sniffed his carrot nose
And said, "At least I'll try,"
And he bravely smiled his frosty smile
And blinked his coal-black eye.
And there he stood and faced the sun
A blazin' from the sky –
And I really cannot tell you
If he ever saw July.
Did he ever see July? You can guess as well as I
If he ever, if he never, if he ever saw July.

Green Winter
Leonard Clark

A green winter, snow
in some ditches though stubbornly lingers,
very first primroses show,
grass pushes up new fingers,
window-panes carved still with frost triangles,
from branch to branch chaffinches flit,
here and there a catkin dangles,
and every blue and long-tailed tit
pretends to be a clown,
pecking at rind and nut,
viewing the garden upside down,
ice splinters now in each water-butt.

Then suddenly overnight
The golden surprise of one aconite.

At Middle-Field Gate in February
Thomas Hardy

The bars are thick with drops that show
    As they gather themselves from the fog
Like silver buttons ranged in a row,
And as evenly spaced as if measured, although
    They fall at the feeblest jog.

They load the leafless hedge hard by,
    And the blades of last year's grass,
While the fallow ploughland turned up nigh
In raw rolls, clammy and clogging lie –
    Too clogging for feet to pass.

How dry it was on a far-back day
    When straws hung the hedge and around,
When amid the sheaves in amorous play
In curtained bonnets and light array
    Bloomed a bevy now underground!

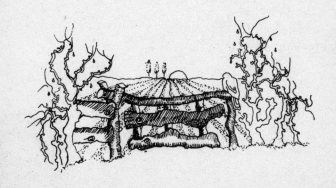

Spring is like a perhaps hand

e. e. cummings

Spring is like a perhaps hand
(which comes carefully
out of Nowhere) arranging
a window, into which people look (while
people stare
arranging and changing placing
carefully there a strange
thing and a known thing here) and

changing everything carefully

spring is like a perhaps
Hand in a window
(carefully to
and fro moving New and
Old things, while
people stare carefully
moving a perhaps
fraction of flower here placing
an inch of air there) and

without breaking anything.

All Sorts
Leonard Clark

In March, all sorts of weather.
Winds wait for you round every corner,
Sun shines, hailstones the moment after,
Hoarfrost on gardens, drizzly mornings.

In March, all sorts of colours,
Grey skies and water, violets in woodlands,
Greenfinches on far greener branches,
Speckled trout rising, first butterflies.

In March, all sorts of happenings,
Hedgehogs stroll quietly round the houses,
Rooks squabble, lambs charge at nothing,
Tadpoles grow fatter, evenings longer.

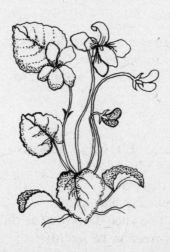

March Morning Unlike Others
Ted Hughes

Blue haze. Bees hanging in air at the hive-mouth.
Crawling in prone stupor of sun
On the hive-lip. Snowdrops. Two buzzards,
Still-wings, each
Magnetised to the other
Float orbits.
Cattle standing warm. Lit, happy stillness.
A raven, under the hill,
Coughing among bare oaks.
Aircraft, elated, splitting blue.
Leisure to stand. The knee-deep mud at the trough
Stiffening. Lambs freed to be foolish.

The earth invalid, dropsied, bruised, wheeled
Out into the sun,
After the frightful operation.
She lies back, wounds undressed to the sun,
To be healed,
Sheltered from the sneapy chill creeping North wind,
Leans back, eyes closed, exhausted, smiling
Into the sun. Perhaps dozing a little.
While we sit, and smile, and wait, and know
She is not going to die.

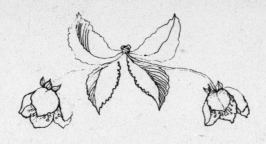

from A Shropshire Lad
A. E. Housman

Loveliest of trees, the cherry now
Is hung with bloom along the bough,
And stands about the woodland ride
Wearing white for Eastertide.

Now, of my threescore years and ten,
Twenty will not come again,
And take from seventy springs a score,
It only leaves me fifty more.

And since to look at things in bloom
Fifty springs are little room,
About the woodlands I will go
To see the cherry hung with snow.

Spring
Gerard Manley Hopkins

Nothing is so beautiful as Spring –
   When weeds, in wheels, shoot long and lovely and lush;
   Thrush's eggs look little low heavens, and thrush
Through the echoing timber does so rinse and wring
The ear, it strikes like lightnings to hear him sing;
   The glassy peartree leaves and blooms, they brush
   The descending blue; that blue is all in a rush
With richness; the racing lambs too have fair their fling.

What is all this juice and all this joy?
   A strain of the earth's sweet being in the beginning
In Eden garden. Have, get, before it cloy,

   Before it cloud, Christ, lord, and sour with sinning,
Innocent mind and Mayday in girl and boy,
   Most, O maid's child, thy choice and worthy the
      winning.

Clouds
Aileen Fisher

Wonder where they come from?
Wonder where they go?
Wonder why they're sometimes high
and sometimes hanging low?
Wonder what they're made of,
and if they weigh a lot?
Wonder if the sky feels bare
up there
    when clouds are not?

from Four Haiku
William Wyatt

A dewy sunrise ...
the birds singing and dancing
on telegraph poles

April Rise
Laurie Lee

If ever I saw blessing in the air
  I see it now in this still early day
Where lemon-green the vaporous morning drips
  Wet sunlight on the powder of my eye.

Blown bubble-film of blue, the sky wraps round
  Weeds of warm light whose every root and rod
Splutters with soapy green, and all the world
  Sweats with the bead of summer in its bud.

If ever I heard blessing it is there
  Where birds in trees that shoals and shadows are
Splash with their hidden wings and drops of sound
  Break on my ears their crests of throbbing air.

Pure in the haze the emerald sun dilates,
  The lips of sparrows milk the mossy stones,
While white as water by the lake a girl
  Swims her green hand among the gathered
    Swans.

Now, as the almond burns its smoking wick,
  Dropping small flames to light the candled grass;
Now, as my low blood scales its second chance,
  If ever world were blessed, now it is.

Summer Farm
Norman MacCaig

Straws like tame lightnings lie about the grass
And hang zigzag on hedges. Green as glass
The water in the horse-trough shines.
Nine ducks go wobbling by in two straight lines.

A hen stares at nothing with one eye,
Then picks it up. Out of an empty sky
A swallow falls and, flickering through
The barn, dives up again into the dizzy blue.

I lie, not thinking, in the cool, soft grass,
Afraid of where a thought might take me – as
This grasshopper with plated face
Unfolds his legs and finds himself in space.

Self under self, a pile of selves I stand
Threaded on time, and with metaphysic hand
Lift the farm like a lid and see
Farm within farm, and in the centre, me.

Poem About the Sun Slinking Off and Pinning Up a Notice
Roger McGough

the sun
hasn't got me fooled
not a minute
just when
you're beginning to believe
that   grass is green
and   skies are blue
and   colour is king
hey   ding a ding ding
and

      a

         host

             of

                  other

                         golden

                              etceteras

before you know where you are
he's slunk off somewhere
and pinned up a notice saying

        MOON

Summer Moods

John Clare

I love at eventide to walk alone
Down narrow lanes oerhung with dewy thorn
Where from the long grass underneath the snail
Jet black creeps out and sprouts his timid horn
I love to muse o'er meadows newly mown
Where withering grass perfumes the sultry air
Where bees search round with sad and weary drone
In vain for flowers that bloomed but newly there
While in the juicey corn the hidden quail
Cries 'wet my foot' and hid as thoughts unborn
The fairy like and seldom-seen land rail
Utters 'craik craik' like voices underground
Right glad to meet the evenings dewy veil
And see the light fade into glooms around

High Summer on the Mountains
Idris Davies

HIGH summer on the mountains
And on the clover leas,
And on the local sidings,
And on the rhubarb leaves.

Brass bands in all the valleys
Blaring defiant tunes,
Crowds, acclaiming carnival,
Prize pigs and wooden spoons

Dust on shabby hedgerows
Behind the colliery wall,
Dust on rail and girder
And tram and prop and all.

High summer on the slag heaps
And on polluted streams,
And old men in the morning
Telling the town their dreams.

The Rainbow

D. H. Lawrence

Even the rainbow has a body
made of the drizzling rain
and is an architecture of glistening atoms
built up, built up
yet you can't lay your hand on it,
nay, nor even your mind.

A Hot Day
A. S. J. Tessimond

Cottonwool clouds loiter.
A lawnmower, very far,
Birrs. Then a bee comes
To a crimson rose and softly
Deftly and fatly crams
A velvet body in.

A tree, June-lazy, makes
A tent of dim green light.
Sunlight weaves in the leaves,
Honey-light laced with leaf-light,
Green interleaved with gold.
Sunlight gathers its rays
In sheaves, which the wind unweaves
And then reweaves – the wind
That puffs a smell of grass
Through the heat-heavy, trembling
Summer pool of air.

Adlestrop

Edward Thomas

Yes. I remember Adlestrop –
The name, because one afternoon
Of heat the express-train drew up there
Unwontedly. It was late June.

The steam hissed. Someone cleared his throat.
No one left and no one came
On the bare platform. What I saw
Was Adlestrop – only the name

And willows, willow-herb, and grass,
And meadowsweet, and haycocks dry,
No whit less still and lonely fair
Than the high cloudlets in the sky.

And for that minute a blackbird sang
Close by, and round him, mistier,
Farther and farther, all the birds
Of Oxfordshire and Gloucestershire.

Tall Nettles
Edward Thomas

Tall nettles cover up, as they have done
These many springs, the rusty harrow, the plough
Long worn out, and the roller made of stone:
Only the elm butt tops the nettles now.

This corner of the farmyard I like most:
As well as any bloom upon a flower
I like the dust on the nettles, never lost
Except to prove the sweetness of a shower.

The Golden Boy
Ted Hughes

In March he was buried
    And nobody cried
Buried in the dirt
    Nobody protested
Where grubs·and insects
    That nobody knows
With outer-space faces
    That nobody loves
Can make him their feast
    As if nobody cared.

But the Lord's mother
    Full of her love
Found him underground
    And wrapped him with love
As if he were her baby
    Her own born love
She nursed him with miracles
    And starry love
And he began to live
    And to thrive on her love

He grew night and day
    And his murderers were glad
He grew like a fire
    And his murderers were happy
He grew lithe and tall
    And his murderers were joyful

He toiled in the fields
               And his murderers cared for him
He grew a gold beard
            And his murderers laughed.

With terrible steel
             They slew him in the furrow
With terrible steel
             They beat his bones from him
With terrible steel
             They ground him to powder
They baked him in ovens
             They sliced him on tables
They ate him they ate him
             They ate him they ate him

Thanking the Lord
Thanking the Wheat
Thanking the Bread
For bringing them Life
Today and Tomorrow
Out of the dirt.

Late Autumn
Andrew Young

The boy called to his team
  And with blue-glancing share
Turned up the rape and turnip
  With yellow charlock to spare.

The long lean thistles stood
  Like beggars ragged and blind,
Half their white silken locks
  Blown away on the wind.

But I thought not once of winter
  Or summer that was past
Till I saw that slant-legged robin
  With autumn on his chest.

Glass Falling
Louis MacNeice

The glass is going down. The sun
Is going down. The forecasts say
It will be warm, with frequent showers.
We ramble down the showery hours
And amble up and down the day.
Mary will wear her black goloshes
And splash the puddles on the town;
And soon on fleets of macintoshes
The rain is coming down, the frown
Is coming down of heaven showing
A wet night coming, the glass is going
Down, the sun is going down.

When the Frost is on the Punkin
James Whitcomb Riley

When the frost is on the punkin and the fodder's in the
  shock,
And you hear the kyouck and gobble of the struttin'
  turkey-cock,
And the clackin' of the guineys, and the cluckin' of the
  hens,
And the rooster's hallylooer as he tiptoes on the fence;

O, it's then's the times a feller is a-feelin' at his best,
With the risin' sun to greet him from a night of peaceful
rest,
As he leaves the house, bareheaded, and goes out to feed
the stock,
When the frost is on the punkin and the fodder's in the
shock.

They's something kindo' harty-like about the atmusfere
When the heat of summer's over and the coolin' fall is
here —
Of course we miss the flowers, and the blossums on the
trees,
And the mumble of the hummin'-birds and buzzin' of the
bees;
But the air's so appetizin'; and the landscape through the
haze
Of a crisp and sunny morning of the airly autumn days
Is a pictur' that no painter has the colorin' to mock —
When the frost is on the punkin and the fodder's in the
shock.

The husky, rusty russel of the tossels of the corn,
And the raspin' of the tangled leaves, as golden as the
morn;
The stubble in the furries – kindo' lonesome-like, but still
A-preachin' sermons to us of the barns they growed to fill;
The strawstack in the medder, and the reaper in the
shed;
The hosses in theyr stalls below – the clover overhead! –
O, it sets my hart a-tickin' like the tickin' of a clock,
When the frost is on the punkin and the fodder's in the
shock!

Then your apples all is gethered, and the ones a feller
keeps
Is poured around the celler-floor in red and yeller heaps;
And your cider-makin' 's over, and your wimmern-folks
is through
With their mince and apple-butter, and theyr souse and
saussage, too! . . .
I don't know how to tell it – but ef sich a thing could be
As the Angels wantin' boardin', and they'd call around
on *me* –
I'd want to 'commodate 'em – all the whole-indurin'
flock –
When the frost is on the punkin and the fodder's in the
shock!

Rain
George MacBeth

wh
en
t   w
he   e
r   ar
ai   e
n   in
is   cl
f   in
al   ed
li   t
ng   o
i   fo
n   rg
lo   et
ng   w
c   ha
ol   t
um   a
ns   mi
       ra
       cl
       e
       it
       i
       s.

It Rains
Edward Thomas

It rains, and nothing stirs within the fence
Anywhere through the orchard's untrodden, dense
Forest of parsley. The great diamonds
Of rain on the grassblades there is none to break,
Or the fallen petals further down to shake.

And I am nearly as happy as possible
To search the wilderness in vain though well,
To think of two walking, kissing there,
Drenched, yet forgetting the kisses of the rain:
Sad, too, to think that never, never again,

Unless alone, so happy shall I walk
In the rain. When I turn away, on its fine stalk
Twilight has fined to naught, the parsley flower
Figures, suspended still and ghostly white,
The past hovering as it revisits the light.

Storm

Roger McGough

They're at it again
the wind and the rain
It all started
when the wind
took the window
by the collar
and shook it
with all its might
Then the rain
butted in
What a din
they'll be at it all night
Serves them right
if they go home in the morning
and the sky won't let them in

Storm in the Black Forest
D. H. Lawrence

Now it is almost night, from the bronzey soft sky
jugfull after jugfull of pure white liquid fire, bright white
tipples over and spills down,
and is gone
and gold-bronze flutters bent through the thick upper air.

And as the electric liquid pours out, sometimes
a still brighter white snake wriggles among it, spilled
and tumbling wriggling down the sky:
and then the heavens cackle with uncouth sounds.

And the rain won't come, the rain refuses to come!

This is the electricity that man is supposed to have
    mastered
chained, subjugated to his use!
supposed to!

Rainy Nights
Irene Thompson

I like the town on rainy nights
    When everything is wet –
When all the town has magic lights
    And streets of shining jet!

When all the rain about the town
    Is like a looking-glass,
And all the lights are upside-down
    Below me as I pass.

In all the pools are velvet skies,
    And down the dazzling street
A fairy city gleams and lies
    In beauty at my feet.

Thunder and Lightning
James Kirkup

Blood punches through every vein
As lightning strips the windowpane.

Under its flashing whip, a white
Village leaps to light.

On tubs of thunder, fists of rain
Slog it out of sight again.

Blood punches the heart with fright
As rain belts the village night.

Something Told the Wild Geese
Rachel Field

Something told the wild geese
   It was time to go.
Though the field lay golden
   Something whispered, 'Snow.'
Leaves were green and stirring,
   Berries, lustre-glossed,
But beneath warm feathers
   Something cautioned, 'Frost.'
All the sagging orchards
   Steamed with amber spice,
But each wild breast stiffened
   At remembered ice.
Something told the wild geese
   It was time to fly –
Summer sun was on their wings,
   Winter in their cry.

Haiku

J. W. Hackett

A bitter morning:
   sparrows sitting together
     without any necks.

Rain drums on the pane
   and runs down, wavering the world
     into a dream.

What the Wind Said
Russell Hoban

"Far away is where I've come from," said the wind.
"Guess what I've brought you."
   "What?" I asked.
"Shadows dancing on a brown road by an old
Stone fence," the wind said. "Do you like that?"
   "Yes," I said. "What else?"
"Daisies nodding, and the drone of one small airplane
In a sleepy sky," the wind continued.
   "I like the airplane, and the daisies too," I said.
   "What else!"
"That's not enough?" the wind complained.
   "No," I said. "I want the song that you were singing.
   Give me that."
"That's mine," the wind said. "Find your own." And left.

Wind

Ted Hughes

This house has been far out at sea all night,
The woods crashing through darkness, the booming hills,
Winds stampeding the fields under the window
Floundering black astride and blinding wet

Till day rose; then under an orange sky
The hills had new places, and wind wielded
Blade-like, luminous black and emerald,
Flexing like the lens of a mad eye.

At noon I scaled along the house-side as far as
The coal-house door. I dared once to look up –
Through the brunt wind that dented the balls of my eyes
The tent of the hills drummed and strained its guyrope,

The fields quivering, the skyline a grimace,
At any second to bang and vanish with a flap:
The wind flung a magpie away and a black-
Back gull bent like an iron bar slowly. The house

Rang like some fine green goblet in the note
That any second would shatter it. Now deep
In chairs, in front of the great fire, we grip
Our hearts and cannot entertain book, thought,

Or each other. We watch the fire blazing,
And feel the roots of the house move, but sit on,
Seeing the window tremble to come in,
Hearing the stones cry out under the horizons.

Winds light to disastrous
Spike Milligan

As I sipped morning tea,
A gale (force three)
Blew away a slice of toast.
Then a gale (force four)
Blew my wife out the door,

I wonder which I'll miss the most.
She was still alive
When a gale (force five)
Blew her screaming o'er Golders Green,
When a gale six blew
And it took her to
A mosque in the Medanine.
Now I pray to heaven
That a gale (force seven)
Will whisk her farther still,*
Let a gale (force eight)
Land her on the plate
Of a cannibal in Brazil.
As I sat down to dine
A gale (force Nine)
Blew away my chips & Spam
But! a gale (force ten)
Blew them back again,
What a lucky man I am!

Bayswater
1977

* Father Still, a stationery priest

Fog

Carl Sandburg

The fog comes
on little cat feet.
It sits looking
over harbour and city
on silent haunches
and then moves on.

Early Shift on the Evening Standard News Desk

Adrian Mitchell

Fog Chaos Grips South

A thick blanket of fog lay across Southern England this
    morning
like a thick blanket –

'Don't let's call it a thick blanket today Joe, let's call it a
sodden yellow eiderdown.'

'Are you insane?'

The Fog
W. H. Davies

I saw the fog grow thick,
 Which soon made blind my ken;
It makes tall men of boys,
 And giants of tall men.

It clutched my throat, I coughed;
 Nothing was in my head
Except two heavy eyes
 Like balls of burning lead.

And when it grew so black
 That I could know no place,
I lost all judgement then,
 Of distance and of space.

The street lamps and the lights
  Upon the halted cars,
Could either be on earth
  Or be the heavenly stars.

A man passed by me close,
  I asked my way, he said,
'Come, follow me, my friend' –
  I followed where he led.

He rapped the stones in front,
  'Trust me,' he said, 'and come';
I followed like a child –
  A blind man led me home.

After a Medieval Song
Ancient Music

Ezra Pound

Winter is icummen in,
Lhude sing Goddamm,
Raineth drop and staineth slop,
And how the wind doth ramm!
      Sing: Goddamm.

Skiddeth bus and sloppeth us,
An ague hath my ham.
Freezeth river, turneth liver,
      Damn you, sing: Goddamm.

Goddamm, Goddamm, 'tis why I am, Goddamm,
      So against the winter's balm.
Sing goddamm, damm, sing Goddamm,
Sing goddamm, sing goddamm, DAMN.

Sleet
Norman MacCaig

The first snow was sleet. It swished heavily
Out of a cloud black enough to hold snow.
It was fine in the wind, but couldn't bear to touch
Anything solid. It died a pauper's death.

Now snow – it grins like a maniac in the moon.
It puts a glove on your face. It stops gaps.
It catches your eye and your breath. It settles down
Ponderously crushing trees with its airy ounces.

But today it was sleet, dissolving spiders on
cheekbones,
Being melted spit on the glass, smudging the mind
That humped itself by the fire, turning away
From the ill wind, the sky filthily weeping.

from Seven Winter Haiku
Chris Torrance

this bare tree touches
    me slightly with its sadness:
so far from summer!

two old beggars sit
    with their pipes by a warm fire
cracking their toes

Snow
Edward Thomas

In the gloom of whiteness,
In the great silence of snow,
A child was sighing
And bitterly saying: 'Oh,
They have killed a white bird up there on her nest,
The down is fluttering from her breast!'
And still it fell through that dusky brightness
On the child crying for the bird of the snow.

Winter Morning

Ogden Nash

Winter is the king of showmen,
Turning tree stumps into snow men
And houses into birthday cakes
And spreading sugar over lakes.
Smooth and clean and frosty white,
The world looks good enough to bite.
That's the season to be young,
Catching snowflakes on your tongue.
Snow is snowy when it's snowing
I'm sorry it's slushy when it's going.

Winter Days
Gareth Owen

Biting air
Winds blow
City streets
Under snow

Noses red
Lips sore
Runny eyes
Hands raw

Chimneys smoke
Cars crawl
Piled snow
On garden wall

Slush in gutters
Ice in lanes
Frosty patterns
On window panes

Morning call
Lift up head
Nipped by winter
Stay in bed

The Kitten in the Falling Snow

James Kirkup

The year-old kitten
has never seen snow,
fallen or falling, until now
this late winter afternoon.

He sits with wide eyes
at the firelit window, sees
white things falling
from black trees.

Are they petals, leaves or birds?
They cannot be the cabbage whites
he batted briefly with his paws,
or the puffball seeds in summer grass.

They make no sound, they have no wings
and yet they can whirl and fly around
until they swoop like swallows, and
disappear into the ground.

'Where do they go?' he questions,
with eyes ablaze, following their flight
into black stone. So I put him
out into the yard, to make their acquaintance.

He has to look up at them: when one
blanches his coral nose, he sneezes,
and flicks a few from his whiskers, from
his sharpened ear, that picks up silences.

He catches one on a curled-up paw
and licks it quickly, before
its strange milk fades, then sniffs its ghost,
a wetness, while his black coat

shivers with stars of flickering frost.
He shivers at something else that makes his thin
tail swish, his fur stand on end! 'What's this? ...'
Then he suddenly scoots in to safety

and sits again with wide eyes
at the firelit window, sees
white things falling
from black trees.

Snow in the Suburbs
Thomas Hardy

Every branch big with it,
Bent every twig with it;
Every fork like a white web-foot;
Every street and pavement mute:
Some flakes have lost their way, and grope back upward,
when
Meeting those meandering down they turn and descend
again.
The palings are glued together like a wall,
And there is no waft of wind with the fleecy fall.

A sparrow enters the tree,
Whereon immediately
A snow-lump thrice his own slight size
Descends on him and showers his head and eyes,
And overturns him,
And near inurns him,
And lights on a nether twig, when its brush
Starts off a volley of other lodging lumps with a rush.

The steps are a blanched slope,
Up which, with feeble hope,
A black cat comes, wide-eyed and thin;
And we take him in.

The Snow Man
Wallace Stevens

One must have a mind of winter
To regard the frost and the boughs
Of the pine-trees crusted with snow;

And have been cold a long time
To behold the junipers shagged with ice,
The spruces rough in the distant glitter

Of the January sun; and not to think
Of any misery in the sound of the wind,
In the sound of a few leaves,

Which is the sound of the land
Full of the same wind
That is blowing in the same bare place

For the listener, who listens in the snow,
And, nothing himself, beholds
Nothing that is not there and the nothing that is.

Winter

Walter de la Mare

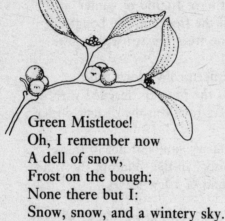

Green Mistletoe!
Oh, I remember now
A dell of snow,
Frost on the bough;
None there but I:
Snow, snow, and a wintery sky.

None there but I,
And footprints one by one,
Zigzaggedly,
Where I had run;
Where shrill and powdery
A robin sat in the tree.

And he whistled sweet;
And I in the crusted snow
With snow-clubbed feet
Jigged to and fro,
Till, from the day,
The rose-light ebbed away.

And the robin flew
Into the air, the air,
The white mist through;
And small and rare
The night-frost fell
Into the calm and misty dell.

And the dusk gathered low,
And the silver moon and stars
On the frozen snow
Drew taper bars,
Kindled winking fires
In the hooded briers.

And the sprawling Bear
Growled deep in the sky;
And Orion's hair
Streamed sparkling by:
But the North sighed low:
'Snow, snow, more snow!'

Winter Ducks
Russell Hoban

Small in the shrink of winter, dark of the frost and chill
Dawnlight beyond my window sill,
I lace the morning stiffly on my feet,
Print bootsteps down the snowy hill to meet
My ducks all waiting where the long black night
Has iced the pond around them. With a spade
I break the water clear; the hole I made
Restores their world to quacking rhyme and reason –
Tails up, they duck the lowering, grey-skied season,
Heads down, they listen to the still-warm song
Of silted leaves and summer, when the days were long.

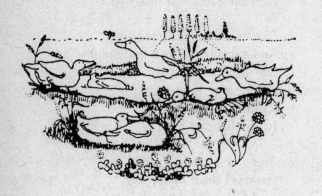

Winter Ocean
John Updike

Many-maned scud-thumper, tub
of male whales, maker of worn wood, shrub-
ruster, sky-mocker, rave!
portly pusher of waves, wind-slave.

Winter Seascape

John Betjeman

The sea runs back against itself
  With scarcely time for breaking wave
To cannonade a slatey shelf
  And thunder under in a cave

Before the next can fully burst.
  The headwind, blowing harder still,
Smooths it to what it was at first –
  A slowly rolling water-hill.

Against the breeze the breakers haste,
  Against the tide their ridges run
And all the sea's a dappled waste
  Criss-crossing underneath the sun.

Far down the beach the ripples drag
   Blown backward, rearing from the shore,
And wailing gull and shrieking shag
   Alone can pierce the ocean roar.

Unheard, a mongrel hound gives tongue,
   Unheard are shouts of little boys:
What chance has any inland lung
   Against this multi-water noise?

Here where the cliffs alone prevail
   I stand exultant, neutral, free,
And from the cushion of the gale
   Behold a huge consoling sea.

Hard Frost
Andrew Young

Frost called to water 'Halt!'
And crusted the moist snow with sparkling salt;
Brooks, their own bridges, stop,
And icicles in long stalactites drop,
And tench in water-holes
Lurk under gluey glass like fish in bowls.

In the hard-rutted lane
At every footstep breaks a brittle pane,
And twinkling trees ice-bound
Changed into weeping willows, sweep the ground;
Dead boughs take roots in ponds
And ferns on windows shoot their ghostly fronds.

But vainly the fierce frost
Interns poor fish, ranks trees in an armed host,
Hangs daggers from house-eaves
And on the windows ferny ambush weaves;
In the long war grown warmer
The sun will strike him dead and strip his armour.

Snow on the City Three Days Before Christmas

Mitchell Goodman

Out of a snow-
white night sky
the speaking wind
drives whiteness down
to trim grim edges of
the city, to round
them.

In the early morning
thrust and grind
of streets is muffled, men
walk one by one, leaving
tracks to tell of their
passing. The cars are snow-
cars, and silent.

The kids who live on concrete
dig the whiteness, their hands
go into it, shape it, they
are softened by
softness.

Roofs, chimneys, bridges
are blessed with whiteness,
women return with their
shopping bags of innocence,
there is gold light on
white, there is a sense
of holiness in high places
there is something like joy
for a morning
in the puzzled faces.

Christmas Landscape
Laurie Lee

Tonight the wind gnaws
with teeth of glass,
the jackdaw shivers
in caged branches of iron,
the stars have talons.

There is hunger in the mouth
of vole and badger,
silver agonies of breath
in the nostrils of the fox,
ice on the rabbit's paw.

Tonight has no moon,
no food for the pilgrim;
The fruit tree is bare,
the rose bush a thorn
and the ground bitter with stones.

But the mole sleeps, and the hedgehog
lies curled in a womb of leaves,
the bean and the wheat-seed
hug their germs in the earth
and the stream moves under the ice.

Tonight there is no moon,
but a new star opens
like a silver trumpet over the dead.
Tonight in a nest of ruins
the blessed babe is laid.

And the fir tree warms to a bloom of candles,
the child lights his lantern,
stares at his tinselled toy;
our hearts and hearths
smoulder with live ashes.

In the blood of our grief
the cold earth is suckled,
in our agony the womb
convulses its seed,
in the cry of anguish
the child's first breath is born.

Index of Authors and Poems

94

Acknowledgements

The publishers gratefully acknowledge permission to reprint this copyright material:

John Murray (Publishers) Ltd for *Winter Seascape* from The Collected Poems of John Betjeman; Curtis Brown Academic Ltd for *Summer Moods* by John Clare, copyright © Eric Robinson 1967; Hodder and Stoughton Ltd for *Green Winter* from The Singing Tree by Leonard Clark; Dennis Dobson Publishers for *All Sorts* from Four Seasons by Leonard Clark; Granada Publishing Ltd and the Liveright Publishing Corporation for *spring is like a perhaps hand* from The Complete Poems by e. e. cummings; E. Morris for *High Summer on the Mountains* by Idris Davies; Jonathan Cape

Ltd and the Executors of the W. H. Davies Estate for *The Fog* from The Complete Poems of W. H. Davies; the Literary Trustees of Walter de la Mare and The Society of Authors as their representative for *Winter* by Walter de la Mare; Macmillan Publishing Co., Inc., for *Something Told the Wild Geese* from Poems by Rachel Field, copyright 1934; World's Work Ltd for *Clouds* from In the Woods In the Meadow In the Sky by Aileen Fisher © 1965; Mitchell Goodman for *Snow on the City Three Days Before Christmas*; J. W. Hackett for *A bitter morning* and *Rain drums on the pane* from The Way of Haiku: Original Verse in English copyright 1969 by Japan Publications, Inc., Tokyo; World's Work Ltd for *The Pedalling Man, What the Wind Said* and *Winter Ducks* from the Pedalling Man by Russell Hoban © 1968; The Society of Authors as the literary representative of the Estate of A. E. Housman, and Jonathan Cape Ltd, for *Loveliest of trees, the cherry now*; Faber and Faber Ltd for *March Morning Unlike Others* and *The Golden Boy* from Season Songs by Ted Hughes; Faber and Faber Ltd and Harper and Row for *Wind* from the Hawk in the Rain by Ted Hughes; James Kirkup for *The Kitten in the Falling Snow*, and for *Thunder and Lightning* from The Prodigal Son published by Oxford University Press; Laurence Pollinger Ltd and the Estate of the Late Mrs Frieda Lawrence Ravagli for *The Rainbow* and *Storm in the Black Forest* from The Complete Poems of D. H. Lawrence published by William Heinemann Ltd; the author for *April Rise* and *Christmas Landscape* from The Bloom of Candles by Laurie Lee published by John Lehmann Ltd; the author for *Rain* by George Macbeth; Chatto and Windus Ltd for *Summer Farm* from Riding Lights and *Sleet* from Measures by Norman McCaig; Faber and Faber Ltd for *Glass Falling* from the Collected Poems of Louis MacNeice; Jonathan Cape Ltd for *The Fight of the Year* and *Poem about the Sun Slinking off and Pinning up a Notice* from Watchwords and *Storm* from After the merrymaking by Roger McGough; Michael Joseph Ltd for *Winds Light to Disastrous* from Unspun Socks from a Chicken's Laundry by Spike Milligan; Jonathan Cape Ltd for *Early Shift on the Evening Standard News Desk* from Ride the Nightmare by Adrian Mitchell; Curtis Brown Ltd, London, on behalf of the Estate of Ogden Nash, and Little, Brown and Company in association with the Atlantic Monthly Press for *It's Never Fair Weather* from Verses From 1929 On by Ogden Nash, copyright 1933 by the Curtis Publishing Company; Curtis Brown, Ltd, London (on behalf of the Estate of Ogden Nash) and New York for *Winter Morning* copyright © 1961, 1962 by Ogden Nash from The New Nutcracker Suite and other Innocent Verses; the author for *Winter Days* from Salford Road by Gareth Owen published by Kestrel Books; Faber and Faber Ltd for *Ancient Music* from Collected Shorter Poems by Ezra Pound; Harcourt Brace Jovanovitch, Inc., for *Fog* from Chicago Poems by Carl Sandburg copyright 1944 by Carl Sandburg; Harper and Row Publishers, Inc., for *Snowman* from Where the Sidewalk Ends: The Poems and Drawings of Shel Silverstein © copyright 1914 by Shel Silverstein; Faber and Faber Ltd and Alfred A. Knopf, Inc., for *The Snow Man* from The Collected Poems of Wallace Stevens; Hubert Nicholson as the author's literary executor for *A Hot Day* by A. S. J. Tessimond, first published by Autolycus Publications; Evans Brothers Ltd for *Rainy Nights* by Irene Thompson from Come Follow Me; Chris Torrance for *two old beggars sit* and *this bare tree touches* from Seven Winter Haiku, from Children of Albion, ed. Mike Horovitz, published by Penguin Books Ltd; The New Yorker Magazine, Inc., for *Winter Ocean* by John Updike; © 1960 The New Yorker Magazine, Inc.; Martin Secker and Warburg Ltd for *Hard Frost, Last Snow* and *Late Autumn* from The Complete Poems by Andrew Young.

Thanks are also due to Macmillan Ltd, publishers of The Complete Poems of Thomas Hardy; and Faber and Faber Ltd, publishers of The Collected Poems of Edward Thomas, and Myfanwy Thomas, his younger daughter.

Every effort has been made to trace the owners of the copyright material in this book. It is the Editor's belief that all necessary permissions have been obtained, but in the case of any question arising as to the use of any material, the Editor will be pleased to make the necessary corrections in future editions of the book.